D1443250

You are a

MOTHER

like no

OTHER

TO my MOM:
For BELIEVING in my DREAMS even before I did,
& SHOWING ME what it means to be a
STRONG-WILLED WOMAN in this world.

Published by Sellers Publishing, Inc.

Copyright © 2019 Sellers Publishing, Inc.

Illustrations © 2019 Becca Cahan

Sellers Publishing, Inc.
161 John Roberts Road, South Portland, Maine 04106
Visit our website: www.sellerspublishing.com ● E-mail: rsp@rsvp.com

Mary L. Baldwin, Managing Editor

Charlotte Cromwell, Production Editor

ISBN 13: 978-1-4162-4668-8

10 9 8 7 6 5 4 3 2 1

Printed in China.

You are a

MOTHER

like no

OTHER

illustrated by
BECCA CAHAN

SELLERS
PUBLISHING

you were my comfort.

My source of

STRENGTH,

my guardian angel.

Your hand was always there
to enfold mine, to

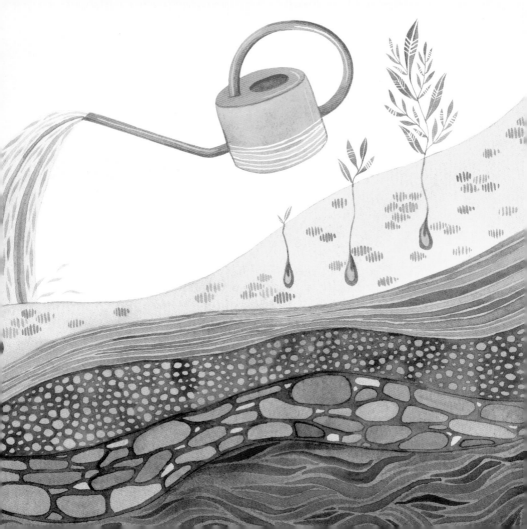

that grew into the
garden where I spent

MY CHILDHOOD.

You stood by the garden's gate
and watched over me to

KEEP
me
SAFE

while I learned to cultivate my dreams.

You loved me enough to

FORGIVE ME

when I was selfish.

You were
COURAGEOUS
enough to allow me to take risks.

YOU FOUND

THE

GOOD in ME

even during times when
I couldn't find it in myself.

YOU **LOVED** ME

without any conditions.

When the time came for me to leave, you

WALKED WITH ME
TO THE DOOR.

Then sent me
ON MY WAY
with a tear, a smile,
and a blessing.

And while I told myself
I was ready to face the world
ON MY OWN.

I knew in my

heart

that if I faltered, you would

BE THERE FOR ME.

And I did falter,
and you were always
there for me,
TO LISTEN &

TO SOOTHE.

Yet when I came to you feeling WEAK, or DISCOURAGED, or DEFEATED, you didn't try to fix me.

You were wise enough to understand that what I needed from you was

SANCTUARY

from the world while I fixed myself.

I am old enough now to grasp

— HOW MUCH —

you have

DONE for ME.

You have given me many gifts
during the course of my life. And

BECAUSE OF
you

I've come to understand the importance
of giving back to others, and listening to,
and believing in, myself.

You taught me that
TO BE HAPPY,
I must live up to my
own ideals.

I marvel at your unflagging
devotion, and reflect on the
myriad of ways you have
influenced the person
I've become, and feel

the
VASTNESS
of your
LOVE

Your faith in me has given me the

STRENGTH.

CONFIDENCE

to endure.

Your guidance has given me the tools to

SUCCEED.

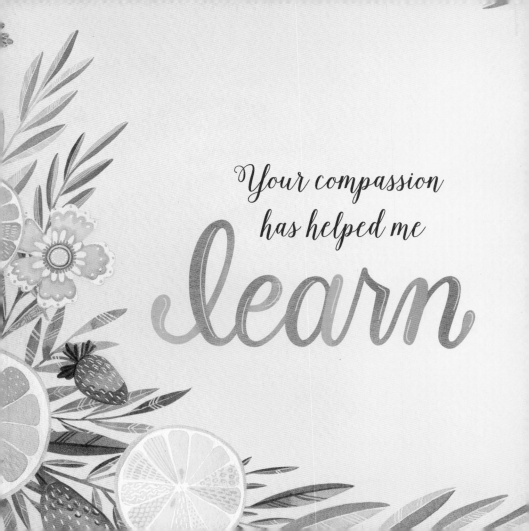

Your compassion
has helped me

learn

to care.

RIGHT&
fair
&TRUE.

Most importantly,

I know what it

means to love

Because you have shown me
what LOVE means.

I will be forever moved, and

for

ever

grateful, for all you've given me.

FORTUNATE
I am to have you
IN MY LIFE.

How fortunate
I am to have you, a

MOTHER

like

NO

OTHER